Simandl

30 ETUDES FOR THE STRING BASS

Published in 2019 by Allegro Editions

30 Etudes for the String Bass
ISBN: 978-1-9748-9999-9 (paperback)

Cover design by Kaitlyn Whitaker

Cover image: "*Double-bass*" by the palms courtesy of Shutterstock;
"*Music Sheet*" by danielo courtesy of Shutterstock

ALLEGRO
EDITIONS

CONTENTS

		Page
ETUDE 1.	Maestoso, in C major (4/4)	3
" 2.	Andante con moto, in F major (3/4)	4
" 3.	Marciale, in Bb major (4/4)	4
" 4.	Allegro ma non troppo, in Eb major (3/4)	6
" 5.	Allegro maestoso, in A minor (4/4)	7
" 6.	Allegro ma non troppo, in A major (4/4, C, 4/4)	8
" 7.	Andante comodo, in G major (3/4)	9
" 8.	Allegro moderato, in G minor (C)	10
" 9.	Moderato, in E major (12/8)	11
" 10.	Moderato maestoso, in C minor (4/4)	12
" 11.	Allegro scherzando, in A minor (6/8)	13
" 12.	Moderato quasi andante, in Ab major (4/4)	14
" 13.	Maestoso assai, in Eb minor (C)	15
" 14.	Maestoso molto pesante, in B major (3/2)	16
" 15.	Andantino, in B minor (3/4, 6/4, 3/4)	17
" 16.	Allegro marcato, in Bb major (4/4)	18
" 17.	Tempo di Polacca, in E minor (3/4)	19
" 18.	Allegro maestoso, in E major (4/4, 3/4, 4/4)	20
" 19.	Largo, in C# minor (3/2)	21
" 20.	Moderato assai, in F major (6/8)	22
" 21.	Risoluto, in F minor (3/4)	23
" 22.	Andante, in Db major (3/4, 5/4, 2/4, 3/4)	24
" 23.	Larghetto, in G# minor (4/4)	25
" 24.	Allegretto, in Gb major (6/8)	26
" 25.	Allegro pesante, in D minor (4/4)	27
" 26.	Grave, in D major (3/4)	28
" 27.	Lento, in F# major (2/4)	29
" 28.	Allegretto moderato, in Bb minor (3/4)	30
" 29.	Andante con moto, in F# minor (3/4)	32
" 30.	Allegro, in E minor (4/4)	34

THIRTY ETUDES
for the
STRING BASS
by
FRANZ SIMANDL

In the study of these Etudes stress is to be laid on the breadth of tone, precision of rhythm and correct intonation (particularly on the A and E strings).

Preceding the study of each Etude it is suggested that the scale of the key in which it is written be played through with the various bowings.

The Etudes are arranged in progressive order and should be practised slowly at first.

Andante comodo. 𝅗𝅥 = 84.

7.

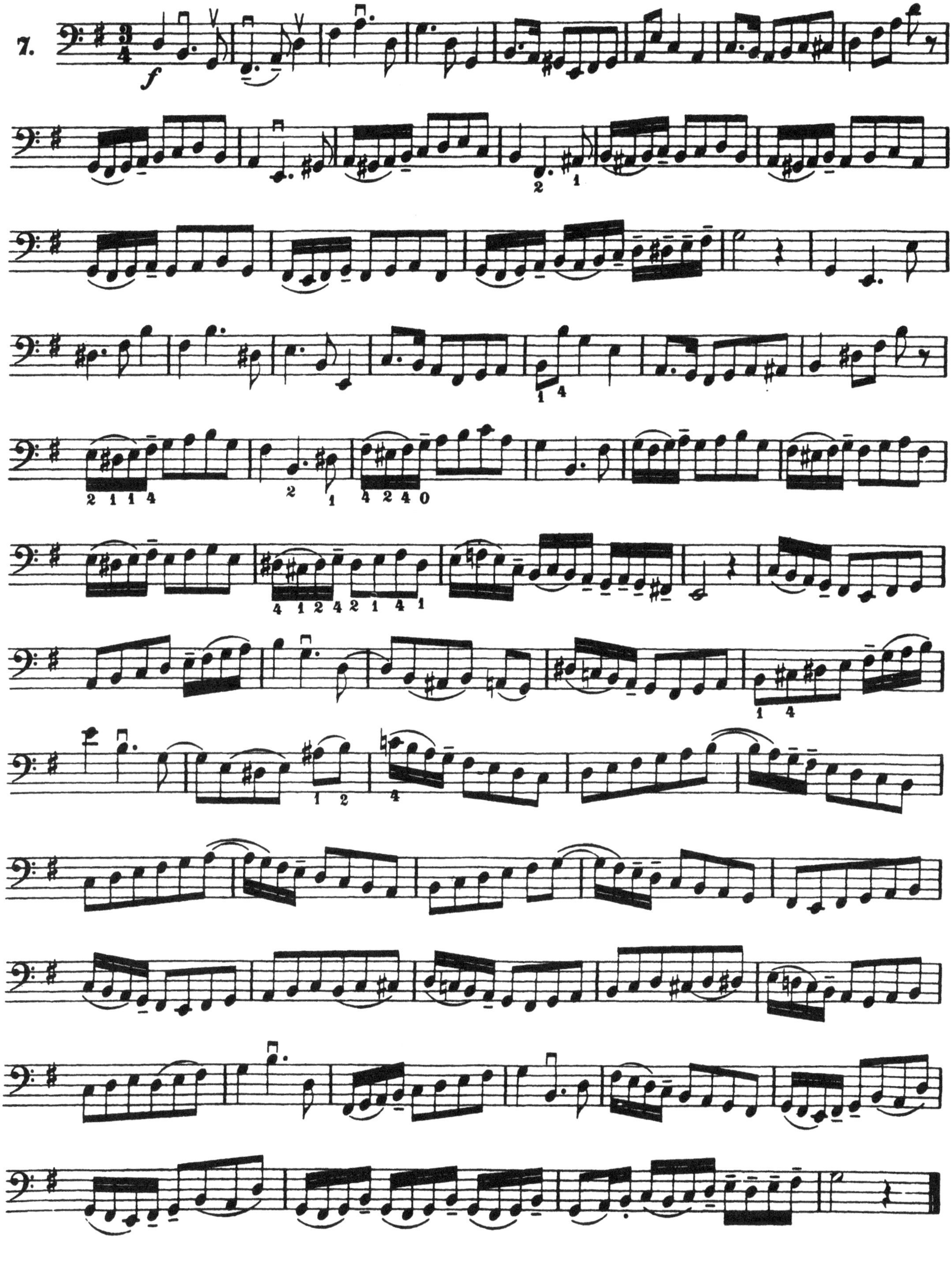

14

Moderato quasi Andante. ♩=96.

16

Maestoso molto pesante. ♩=72.

14.

20

21

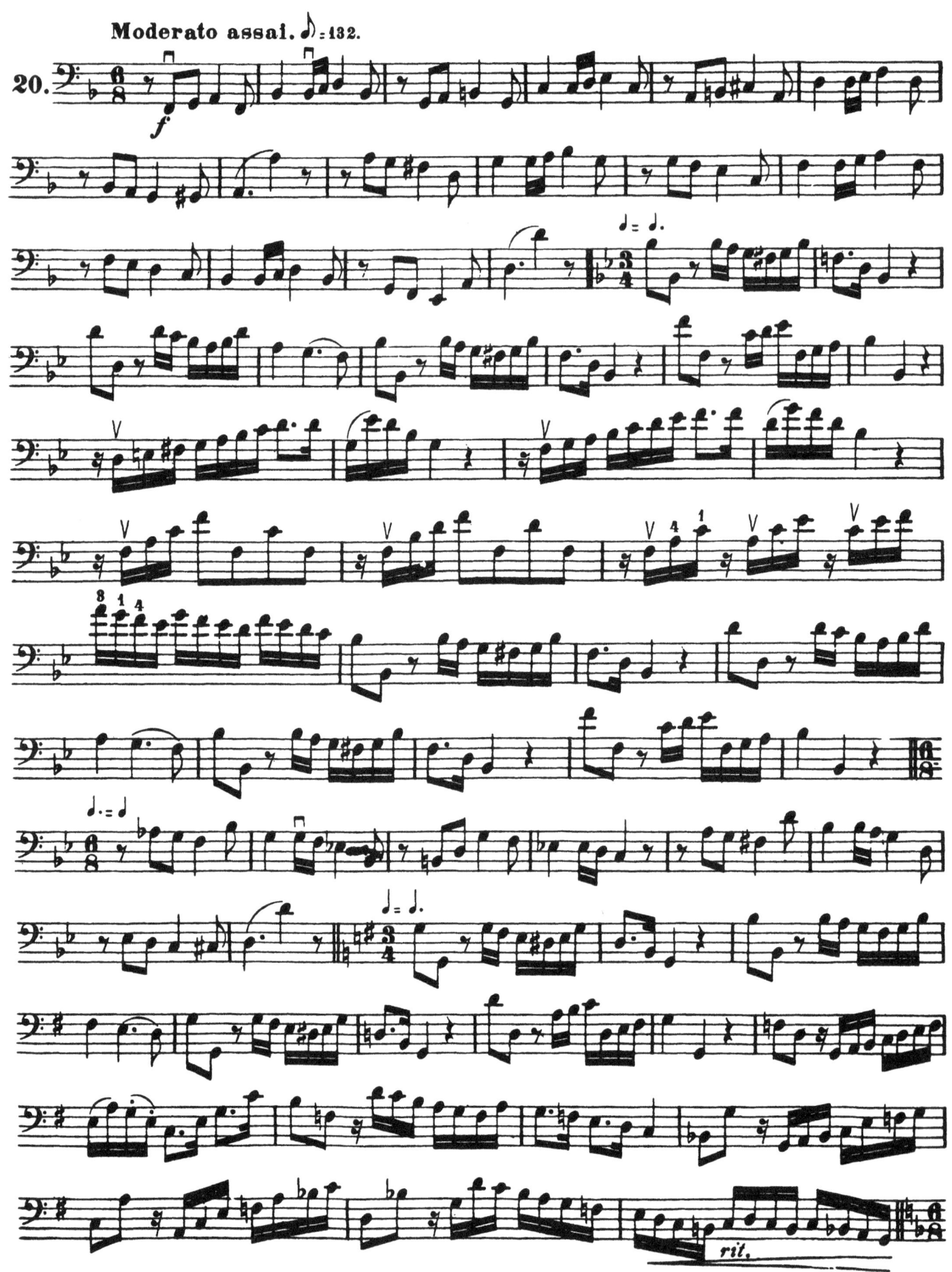

35

www.ingramcontent.com/pod-product-compliance
Lightning Source LLC
Chambersburg PA
CBHW081357040426
42451CB00017B/3480